Take Up the Song

Dec. 2, 1986

Dear Elizabeth —
    A letter, a bicycle ride + picnic,
a concert in a castle, that walk
along the beach. — — — — — — . . . .
                        Love, Ivan

Take Up the Song

Poems by
Edna St. Vincent Millay

Photographs by
Ivan Massar

Edited by Ivan Massar

1817

HARPER & ROW, PUBLISHERS, New York
Cambridge, Philadelphia, San Francisco, Washington,
London, Mexico City, São Paulo, Singapore, Sydney

Grateful acknowledgment is made to Norma Millay Ellis for permission
to reprint poems from the following Edna St. Vincent Millay collections originally published
by Harper & Row, Publishers:

THE BUCK IN THE SNOW. Copyright, 1928, by Edna St. Vincent Millay. Copyright renewed 1956 by Norma Millay Ellis.

THE HARP-WEAVER. Copyright, 1920, 1921, 1922, 1923 by Edna St. Vincent Millay. Copyright renewed 1948, 1949, 1950 by Edna St. Vincent Millay, 1951 by Norma Millay Ellis.

RENASCENCE. Copyright, 1917, by Edna St. Vincent Millay. Copyright renewed 1945 by Edna St. Vincent Millay.

WINE FROM THESE GRAPES. Copyright, 1934, by Edna St. Vincent Millay. Copyright renewed 1962 by Norma Millay Ellis.

SECOND APRIL. Copyright, 1918, 1919, 1920, 1921 by Edna St. Vincent Millay. Copyright renewed 1946, 1947, 1948, 1949 by Edna St. Vincent Millay.

COLLECTED POEMS. Copyright © 1956 by Norma Millay Ellis. Copyright renewed 1984 by Norma Millay Ellis.

MINE THE HARVEST. Copyright, 1941, by Edna St. Vincent Millay. Copyright, 1945, 1946, 1947, 1952, 1953, 1954 by Norma Millay Ellis. Copyright, 1945, by Curtis Publishing Company. Copyright renewed 1969, 1973, 1974, 1975, 1977, 1980, 1982 by Norma Millay Ellis.

A FEW FIGS FROM THISTLES. Copyright, 1922, by Edna St. Vincent Millay. Copyright renewed 1950 by Edna St. Vincent Millay.

HUNTSMAN, WHAT QUARRY? Copyright, 1933, 1934, 1936, 1937, 1938, 1939 by Edna St. Vincent Millay. Copyright renewed 1961, 1962, 1964, 1965, 1966, 1967 by Norma Millay Ellis.

FATAL INTERVIEW. Copyright, 1931 by Edna St. Vincent Millay. Copyright renewed 1959 by Norma Millay Ellis.

TAKE UP THE SONG

FIRST EDITION

Design: Jeannie Abbott

Typography: Garbo Typesetting

Printing: Grafiche Milani

Library of Congress Catalog Card Number: 86-45129
ISBN: 0-06-015461-6

To Mom and Dad

whose love of nature started me
looking at an early age

To Norma Millay Ellis for generosity and hospitality during the many visits to Austerlitz to photograph and discuss the book. I shall always treasure the memory of the hours spent looking at photographs with her spontaneous and eloquent recitation of her sister's poetry.

To Howard Chapnick for his understanding and patience, and his many valuable contributions toward bringing this project to fruition.

Special thanks: To Beverly Bringle for inspiration and patience during the many months in search of photographs. For their hospitality, friendship, and encouragement: Jan Watson, Marjorie Young, Vanessa, Ramona and all the Barths of Alna, Andrea Massar, David and Andrea Massar, Dzidra Knecht, Sally Reynolds. To Mary King and Anne Perkins for contact with Harper & Row.

Special thanks to Luigi Canton of Grafiche Milani for his special attention and care and for his artistry in printing. For generosity with their professional advice: Jackie Casey, Bruce MacIntosh, Paul Nemoda, Aldo Simonini, Tatul Sonentz-Papazian, Buz Wyeth and Carl Zahn.

To Jeannie Abbott, designer for this book, who in fact has been much more. With a long-standing love of Millay poetry and a deep understanding of my photographs, her contributions to editorial and artistic decisions were invaluable in shaping the book.

CONTENTS

While wandering through my meadow one misty morning, I was making photographs, intoxicated by the magic of the day. Vincent's words came to me:

Here such a passion is
As stretcheth me apart . . . .

I thought, surely scenes such as this one inspired her words and her genius. I found in her poetry a reflection of my own thoughts and images. Finding a particularly beautiful shape or form, or a special quality of light to photograph inspires and excites me. It makes me think of her passion for life and living expressed in her poetry.

Though I may photograph a rock, reeds in the water or shadows and reflections, what I experience is beyond these realities. I feel a mood of sadness over lost love and remembered pain, or the ecstasy of a new day and creative challenge. I stand in awe of the perfection of nature's simple statement and feel pure joy over the balance I see.

My aim is to convey a sense of exhilaration, of exploration within and without, and discovery of new worlds in each of these newly found jewels. I want to retain my childlike curiosity and enthusiasm for Nature's wonderland.

This book is my effort to *Take Up the Song,* to echo Vincent's lyrics with my images of her beloved coastal Maine, the fields and streams of Concord and the meadows and woodlands of Austerlitz.

Still will I harvest beauty where it grows:
In coloured fungus and the spotted fog.

May this melody of Vincent's poetry with my photographs make a beautiful duet.

Ivan Massar

* * *

Grow not too high, grow not too far from home,
Green tree, whose roots are in the granite's face!
Taller than silver spire or golden dome
A tree may grow above its earthy place,
And taller than a cloud, but not so tall
The root may not be mother to the stem,
Lifting rich plenty, though the rivers fall,
To the cold sunny leaves to nourish them.
Have done with blossoms for a time, be bare;
Split rock; plunge downward; take heroic soil,—
Deeper than bones, no pasture for you there;
Deeper than water, deeper than gold and oil:
Earth's fiery core alone can feed the bough
That blooms between Orion and the Plough.

On First Having Heard the Skylark

Not knowing he rose from earth, not having seen him rise,

Not knowing the fallow furrow was his home,

And that high wing, untouchable, untainted,

A wing of earth, with the warm loam

Closely acquainted,

I shuddered at his cry and caught my heart.

Relentless out of heaven his sweet crying like a crystal dart

Was launched against me. Scanning the empty sky

I stood with thrown-back head until the world reeled.

Still, still he sped his unappeasable shafts against my breast without a shield.

He cried forever from his unseen throat

Between me and the sun.

He would not end his singing, he would not have done.

"Serene and pitiless note, whence, whence are you?"

I cried. "Alas, these arrows, how fast they fall!

Ay, me, beset by angels in unequal fight,

Alone high on the shaven down surprised, and not a tree in sight!"

Even as I spoke he was revealed

Above me in the bright air,

A dark articulate atom in the mute enormous blue,

A mortal bird, flying and singing in the morning there.

Even as I spoke I spied him, and I knew,

And called him by his name;

"Blithe Spirit!" I cried. Transfixed by more than mortal spears

I fell; I lay among the foreign daisies pink and small,

And wept, staining their innocent faces with fast-flowing tears.

Northern April

O mind, beset by music never for a moment quiet, —
The wind at the flue, the wind strumming the shutter;
The soft, antiphonal speech of the doubled brook,
    never for a moment quiet;
The rush of the rain against the glass, his voice in the eaves-gutter!

Where shall I lay you to sleep, and the robins be quiet?
Lay you to sleep — and the frogs be silent in the marsh?
Crashes the sleet from the bough and the bough sighs upward,
    never for a moment quiet.
April is upon us, pitiless and young and harsh.

O April, full of blood, full of breath, have pity upon us!
Pale, where the winter like a stone has been lifted away,
    we emerge like yellow grass.
Be for a moment quiet, buffet us not, have pity upon us,
Till the green come back into the vein, till the giddiness pass.

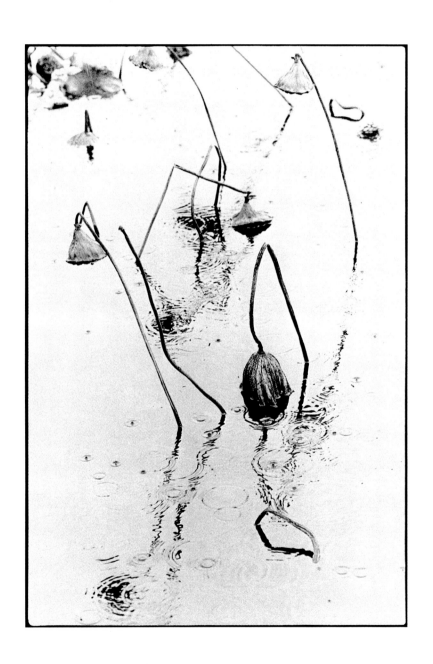

On Hearing a Symphony of Beethoven

Sweet sounds, oh, beautiful music, do not cease!
Reject me not into the world again.
With you alone is excellence and peace,
Mankind made plausible, his purpose plain.
Enchanted in your air benign and shrewd,
With limbs a-sprawl and empty faces pale,
The spiteful and the stingy and the rude
Sleep like the scullions in the fairy-tale.
This moment is the best the world can give:
The tranquil blossom on the tortured stem.
Reject me not, sweet sounds! oh, let me live,
Till Doom espy my towers and scatter them.
A city spell-bound under the aging sun,
Music my rampart, and my only one.

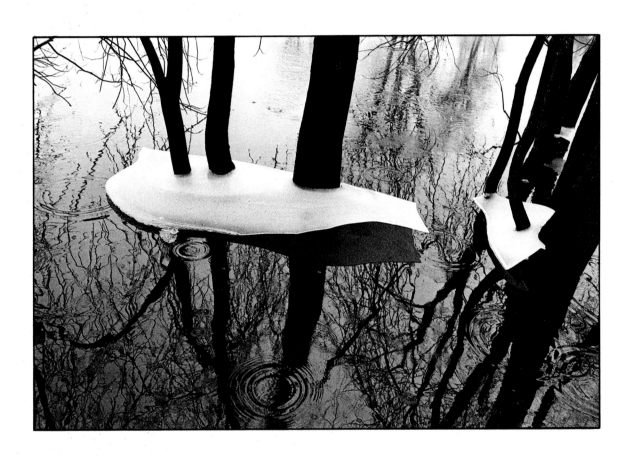

*   *   *

Pity me not because the light of day
At close of day no longer walks the sky;
Pity me not for beauties passed away
From field and thicket as the year goes by;
Pity me not the waning of the moon,
Nor that the ebbing tide goes out to sea,
Nor that a man's desire is hushed so soon,
And you no longer look with love on me.
This have I known always: Love is no more
Than the wide blossom which the wind assails,
Than the great tide that treads the shifting shore,
Strewing fresh wreckage gathered in the gales:
Pity me that the heart is slow to learn
What the swift mind beholds at every turn.

*   *   *

Still will I harvest beauty where it grows:
In coloured fungus and the spotted fog
Surprised on foods forgotten; in ditch and bog
Filmed brilliant with irregular rainbows
Of rust and oil, where half a city throws
Its empty tins; and in some spongy log
Whence headlong leaps the oozy emerald frog. . . .
And a black pupil in the green scum shows.
Her the inhabiter of divers places
Surmising at all doors, I push them all.
Oh, you that fearful of a creaking hinge
Turn back forevermore with craven faces,
I tell you Beauty bears an ultra fringe
Unguessed of you upon her gossamer shawl!

Afternoon on a Hill

I will be the gladdest thing
    Under the sun!
I will touch a hundred flowers
    And not pick one.

I will look at cliffs and clouds
    With quiet eyes,
Watch the wind bow down the grass,
    And the grass rise.

And when lights begin to show
    Up from the town,
I will mark which must be mine,
    And then start down!

The Fawn

There it was I saw what I shall never forget
And never retrieve.
Monstrous and beautiful to human eyes, hard to believe,
He lay, yet there he lay,
Asleep on the moss, his head on his polished cleft small ebony hooves,
The child of the doe, the dappled child of the deer.

Surely his mother had never said, "Lie here
Till I return," so spotty and plain to see
On the green moss lay he.
His eyes had opened; he considered me.

I would have given more than I care to say
To thrifty ears, might I have had him for my friend
One moment only of that forest day:

Might I have had the acceptance, not the love
Of those clear eyes;
Might I have been for him the bough above
Or the root beneath his forest bed,
A part of the forest, seen without surprise.

Was it alarm, or was it the wind of my fear lest he depart
That jerked him to his jointy knees,
And sent him crashing off, leaping and stumbling
On his new legs, between the stems of the white trees?

God's World

O world, I cannot hold thee close enough!
  Thy winds, thy wide grey skies!
  Thy mists, that roll and rise!
Thy woods, this autumn day, that ache and sag
And all but cry with colour! That gaunt crag
To crush! To lift the lean of that black bluff!
World, World, I cannot get thee close enough!

Long have I known a glory in it all,
    But never knew I this:
    Here such a passion is
As stretcheth me apart, — Lord, I do fear
Thou'st made the world too beautiful this year;
My soul is all but out of me, — let fall
No burning leaf; prithee, let no bird call.

Assault

I had forgotten how the frogs must sound
After a year of silence, else I think
I should not so have ventured forth alone
At dusk upon this unfrequented road.

I am waylaid by Beauty. Who will walk
Between me and the crying of the frogs?
Oh, savage Beauty, suffer me to pass,
That am a timid woman, on her way
From one house to another!

(From an unfinished poem)

As sharp as in my childhood, still
Ecstasy shocks me fixed. The will
Cannot entice it, never could,
So never tries. But for the wood
The wind will hurl the clashing sleet;
Or a small fawn with lovely feet,
Uncertain in its gait, will walk
Among the ferns, not breaking back
One frond, not bruising one fern black,
Into the clearing, and appraise
With mild, attracted, wondering gaze,
And lifted head unhurt and new,
This world that he was born into.

Such marvels as, one time, I feared
Might go, and leave me unprepared
For hardship. But they never did.
They blaze before me still, as wild
And clear, as when I was a child.
They never went away at all.
I need not, though I do, recall
Such moments in my childhod, when
Wonder sprang out at me again,
And took me by the heels, and whirled
Me round and round above the world.

For wonder leaps upon me still,
And makes me dizzy, makes me ill,
But never frightened — for I know —
Not where — but in whose hands I go:
The lovely fingers of Delight
Have hold of me and hold me tight.

*   *   *

How healthily their feet upon the floor
Strike down! These are no spirits, but a band
Of children, surely, leaping hand in hand
Into the air in groups of three and four,
Wearing their silken rags as if they wore
Leaves only and light grasses, or a strand
Of black elusive seaweed oozing sand,
And running hard as if along a shore.
I know how lost forever, and at length
How still these lovely tossing limbs shall lie,
And the bright laughter and the panting breath;
And yet, before such beauty and such strength,
Once more, as always when the dance is high,
I am rebuked that I believe in death.

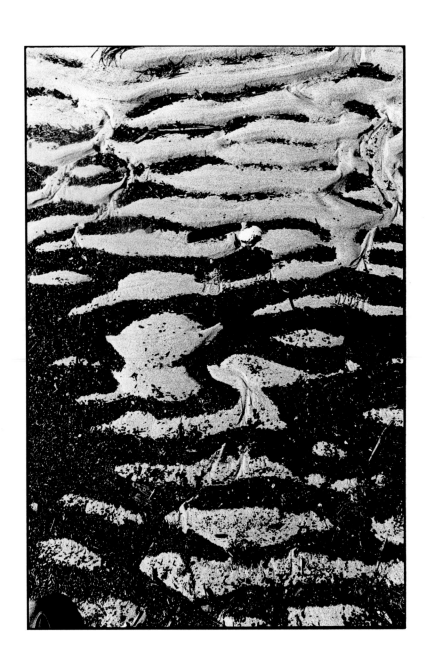

Low-Tide

These wet rocks where the tide has been,
   Barnacled white and weeded brown
And slimed beneath to a beautiful green,
   These wet rocks where the tide went down
Will show again when the tide is high
   Faint and perilous, far from shore,
No place to dream, but a place to die:
   The bottom of the sea once more.

There was a child that wandered through
   A giant's empty house all day, —
House full of wonderful things and new,
   But no fit place for a child to play!

Sonnet to Gath

Country of hunchbacks!—where the strong, straight spine,
Jeered at by crooked children, makes his way
Through by-streets at the kindest hour of day,
Till he deplore his stature, and incline
To measure manhood with a gibbous line;
Till out of loneliness, being flawed with clay,
He stoop into his neighbour's house and say,
"Your roof is low for me—the fault is mine."
Dust in an urn long since, dispersed and dead
Is great Apollo; and the happier he;
Since who amongst you all would lift a head
At a god's radiance on the mean door-tree,
Saving to run and hide your dates and bread,
And cluck your children in about your knee?

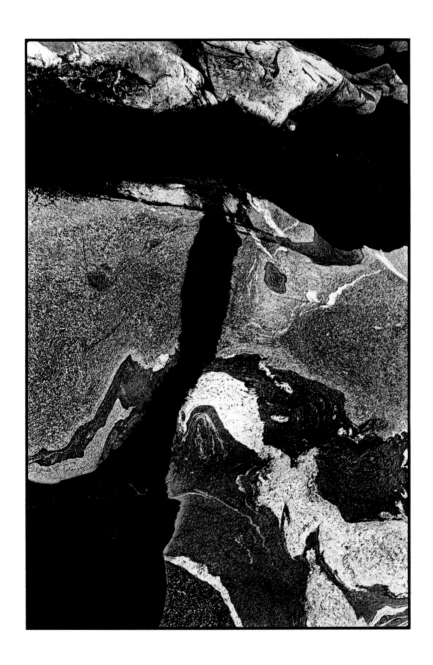

＊　　＊　　＊

We have gone too far; we do not know how to stop: impetus
Is all we have. And we share it with the pushed Inert.

We are clever, — we are as clever as monkeys; and some of us
Have intellect, which is our danger, for we lack intelligence
And have forgotten instinct.

Progress — progress is the dirtiest word in the language — who
    ever told us —
And made us believe it — that to take a step forward was
    necessarily, was always
A good idea?
In this unlighted cave, one step forward
That step can be the down-step into the Abyss.
But we, we have no sense of direction; impetus
Is all we have; we do not proceed, we only
Roll down the mountain,
Like disbalanced boulders, crushing before us many
Delicate springing things, whose plan it was to grow.

Clever, we are, and inventive, — but not creative;

For, to create, one must decide — the cells must decide — what form,

What colour, what sex, how many petals, five, or more than five,

Or less than five.

But we, we decide nothing: the bland Opportunity

Presents itself, and we embrace it, — we are so grateful

When something happens which is not directly War;

For we think — although of course, now, we very seldom

Clearly think —

That the other side of War is Peace.

We have no sense; we only roll downhill. Peace

Is the temporary beautiful ignorance that War

Somewhere progresses.

Read history: so learn your place in Time;

And go to sleep: all this was done before;

We do it better, fouling every shore;

We disinfect, we do not probe, the crime.

Our engines plunge into the seas, they climb

Above our atmosphere: we grow not more

Profound as we approach the ocean's floor;

Our flight is lofty, it is not sublime.

Yet long ago this Earth by struggling men

Was scuffed, was scraped by mouths that bubbled mud;

And will be so again, and yet again;

Until we trace our poison to its bud

And root, and there uproot it: until then,

Earth will be warmed each winter by man's blood.

*   *   *

Read history: thus learn how small a space
You may inhabit, nor inhabit long
In crowding Cosmos—in that confined place
Work boldly; build your flimsy barriers strong;
Turn round and round, make warm your nest; among
The other hunting beasts, keep heart and face,—
Not to betray the doomed and splendid race
You are so proud of, to which you belong.
For trouble comes to all of us: the rat
Has courage, in adversity, to fight;
But what a shining animal is man,
Who knows, when pain subsides, that is not that,
For worse than that must follow—yet can write
Music; can laugh; play tennis; even plan.

Conscientious Objector

I shall die, but that is all that I shall do for Death.

I hear him leading his horse out of the stall; I hear the clatter on the barn-floor.
He is in haste; he has business in Cuba, business in the Balkans,
      many calls to make this morning.
But I will not hold the bridle while he cinches the girth.
And he may mount by himself: I will not give him a leg up.

Though he flick my shoulders with his whip, I will not tell him
      which way the fox ran.
With his hoof on my breast, I will not tell him where the black boy
      hides in the swamp.
I shall die, but that is all that I shall do for Death; I am not
      on his pay-roll.

I will not tell him the whereabouts of my friends nor of my enemies either.
Though he promise me much, I will not map him the route
      to any man's door.
Am I a spy in the land of the living, that I should deliver men to Death?
Brother, the password and the plans of our city are safe with me;
      never through me
Shall you be overcome.

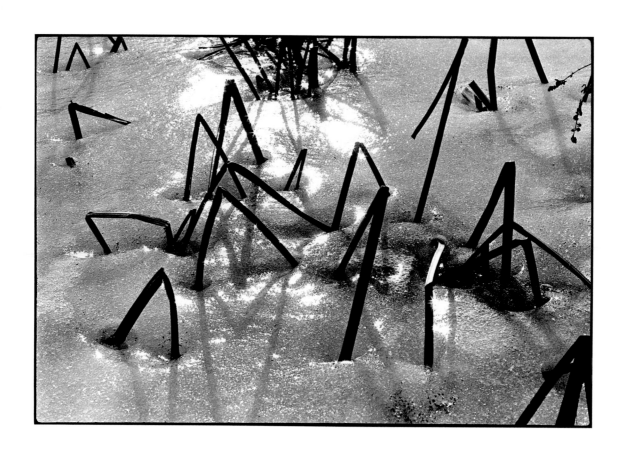

Three Sonnets in Tetrameter

I

See how these masses mill and swarm
And troop and muster and assail:
God! — We could keep this planet warm
By friction, if the sun should fail.
Mercury, Saturn, Venus, Mars:
If no prow cuts your arid seas,
Then in your weightless air no wars
Explode with such catastrophes
As rock our planet all but loose
From its frayed mooring to the sun.
Law will not sanction such abuse
Forever; when the mischief's done,
Planets, rejoice, on which at night
Rains but the twelve-ton meteorite.

II

His stalk the dark delphinium
Unthorned into the tending hand
Releases . . . yet that hour will come . . .
And must, in such a spiny land.
The silky, powdery mignonette
Before these gathering dews are gone
May pierce me — does the rose regret
The day she did her armour on?
In that the foul supplants the fair,
The coarse defeats the twice-refined,
Is food for thought, but not despair:
All will be easier when the mind
To meet the brutal age has grown
An iron cortex of its own.

III

No further from me than my hand
Is China that I loved so well;
Love does not help to understand
The logic of the bursting shell.
Perfect in dream above me yet
Shines the white cone of Fuji-San;
I wake in fear, and weep and sweat . . .
Weep for Yoshida, for Japan.
Logic alone, all love laid by,
Must calm this crazed and plunging star:
Sorrowful news for such as I,
Who hoped — with men just as they are,
Sinful and loving — to secure
A human peace that might endure.

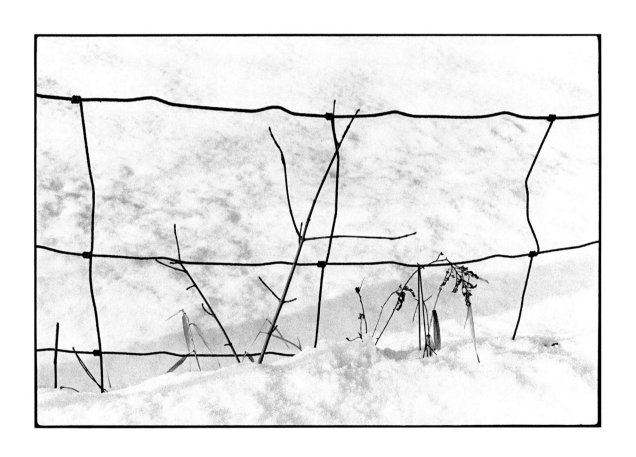

Autumn Chant

Now the autumn shudders
   In the rose's root.
Far and wide the ladders
   Lean among the fruit.

Now the autumn clambers
   Up the trellised frame,
And the rose remembers
   The dust from which it came.

Brighter than the blossom
   On the rose's bough
Sits the wizened, orange,
   Bitter berry now;

Beauty never slumbers;
   All is in her name;
But the rose remembers
   The dust from which it came.

If Still Your Orchards Bear

Brother, that breathe the August air
    Ten thousand years from now,
And smell—if still your orchards bear
    Tart apples on the bough—

The early windfall under the tree,
    And see the red fruit shine,
I cannot think your thoughts will be
    Much different from mine.

Should at that moment the full moon
    Step forth upon the hill,
And memories hard to bear at noon,
    By moonlight harder still,

Form in the shadows of the trees,—
    Things that you could not spare
And live, or so you thought, yet these
    All gone, and you still there,

A man no longer what he was,
    Nor yet the thing he'd planned,
The chilly apple from the grass
    Warmed by your living hand—

I think you will have need of tears;
    I think they will not flow;
Supposing in ten thousand years
    Men ache, as they do now.

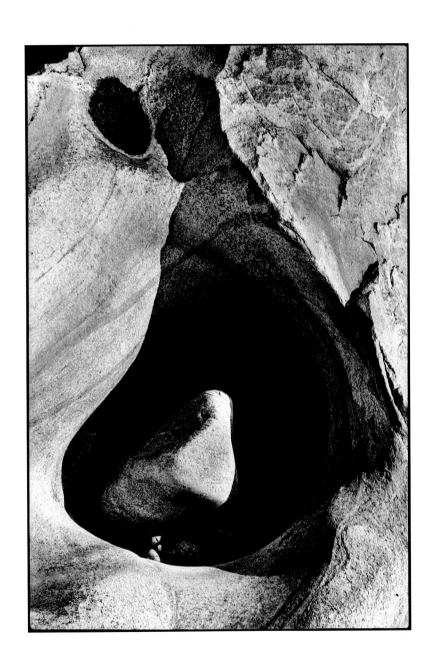

Elegy Before Death

There will be rose and rhododendron
    When you are dead and under ground;
Still will be heard from white syringas
    Heavy with bees, a sunny sound;

Still will the tamaracks be raining
    After the rain has ceased, and still
Will there be robins in the stubble,
    Grey sheep upon the warm green hill.

Spring will not ail nor autumn falter;
    Nothing will know that you are gone, —
Saving alone some sullen plough-land
    None but yourself sets foot upon;

Saving the may-weed and the pig-weed
    Nothing will know that you are dead, —
These, and perhaps a useless wagon
    Standing beside some tumbled shed.

Oh, there will pass with your great passing
    Little of beauty not your own, —
Only the light from common water,
    Only the grace from simple stone!

Song of a Second April

April this year, not otherwise
   Than April of a year ago,
Is full of whispers, full of sighs,
   Of dazzling mud and dingy snow;
   Hepaticas that pleased you so
Are here again, and butterflies.

There rings a hammering all day,
   And shingles lie about the doors;
In orchards near and far away
   The grey wood-pecker taps and bores;
   And men are merry at their chores,
And children earnest at their play.

The larger streams run still and deep,
   Noisy and swift the small brooks run;
Among the mullein stalks the sheep
   Go up the hillside in the sun,
   Pensively,—only you are gone,
You that alone I cared to keep.

Fatal Interview

XXX

Love is not all: it is not meat nor drink
Nor slumber nor a roof against the rain;
Nor yet a floating spar to men that sink
And rise and sink and rise and sink again;
Love can not fill the thickened lung with breath,
Nor clean the blood, nor set the fractured bone;
Yet many a man is making friends with death
Even as I speak, for lack of love alone.
It well may be that in a difficult hour,
Pinned down by pain and moaning for release,
Or nagged by want past resolution's power,
I might be driven to sell your love for peace,
Or trade the memory of this night for food.
It well may be. I do not think I would.

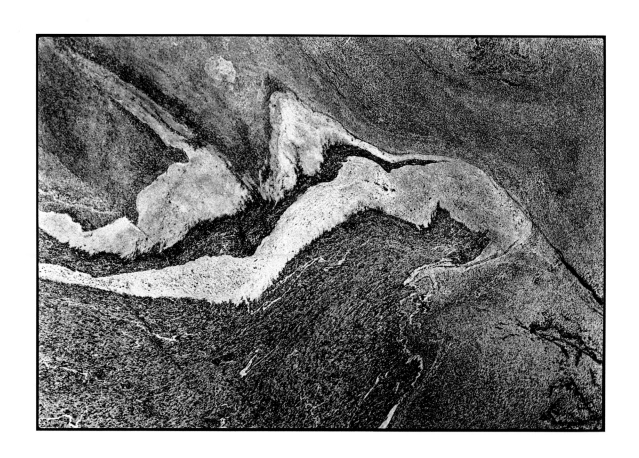

Feast

I drank at every vine.
    The last was like the first.
I came upon no wine
    So wonderful as thirst.

I gnawed at every root.
    I ate of every plant.
I came upon no fruit
    So wonderful as want.

Feed the grape and bean
    To the vintner and monger;
I will lie down lean
    With my thirst and my hunger.

* * *

What lips my lips have kissed, and where, and why,
I have forgotten, and what arms have lain
Under my head till morning; but the rain
Is full of ghosts tonight, that tap and sigh
Upon the glass and listen for reply,
And in my heart there stirs a quiet pain
For unremembered lads that not again
Will turn to me at midnight with a cry.
Thus in the winter stands the lonely tree,
Nor knows what birds have vanished one by one,
Yet knows its boughs more silent than before:
I cannot say what loves have come and gone,
I only know that summer sang in me
A little while, that in me sings no more.

The Leaf and the Tree

When will you learn, my self, to be
A dying leaf on a living tree?
Budding, swelling, growing strong,
Wearing green, but not for long,
Drawing sustenance from air,
That other leaves, and you not there,
May bud, and at the autumn's call
Wearing russet, ready to fall?

Has not this trunk a deed to do
Unguessed by small and tremulous you?
Shall not these branches in the end
To wisdom and the truth ascend?
And the great lightning plunging by
Look sidewise with a golden eye
To glimpse a tree so tall and proud
It sheds its leaves upon a cloud?

Here, I think, is the heart's grief:
The tree, no mightier than the leaf,
Makes firm its root and spreads its crown
And stands; but in the end comes down.
That airy top no boy could climb
Is trodden in a little time
By cattle on their way to drink.
The fluttering thoughts a leaf can think,
That hears the wind and waits its turn,
Have taught it all a tree can learn.

Time can make soft that iron wood.
The tallest trunk that ever stood,
In time, without a dream to keep,
Crawls in beside the root to sleep.

       ❈   ❈   ❈

Time does not bring relief; you all have lied
Who told me time would ease me of my pain!
I miss him in the weeping of the rain;
I want him at the shrinking of the tide;
The old snows melt from every mountain-side,
And last year's leaves are smoke in every lane;
But last year's bitter loving must remain
Heaped on my heart, and my old thoughts abide.
There are a hundred places where I fear
To go,—so with his memory they brim.
And entering with relief some quiet place
Where never fell his foot or shone his face
I say, "There is no memory of him here!"
And so stand stricken, so remembering him.

Dirge Without Music

I am not resigned to the shutting away of loving hearts in the hard ground.
So it is, and so it will be, for so it has been, time out of mind:
Into the darkness they go, the wise and the lovely. Crowned
With lilies and with laurel they go; but I am not resigned.

Lovers and thinkers, into the earth with you.
Be one with the dull, the indiscriminate dust.
A fragment of what you felt, of what you knew,
A formula, a phrase remains,—but the best is lost.

The answers quick and keen, the honest look, the laughter, the love,—
They are gone. They are gone to feed the roses. Elegant and curled
Is the blossom. Fragrant is the blossom. I know. But I do not approve.
More precious was the light in your eyes than all the roses in the world.

Down, down, down into the darkness of the grave
Gently they go, the beautiful, the tender, the kind;
Quietly they go, the intelligent, the witty, the brave.
I know. But I do not approve. And I am not resigned.

Aubade

Cool and beautiful as the blossom of the wild carrot
With its crimson central eye,
Round and beautiful as the globe of the onion blossom
Were her pale breasts whereon I laid me down to die.

From the wound of my enemy that thrust me through in the dark wood
I arose; with sweat on my lip and the wild woodgrasses in my spur
I arose and stood.
But never did I arise from loving her.

* * *

I know I am but summer to your heart,
And not the full four seasons of the year;
And you must welcome from another part
Such noble moods as are not mine, my dear.
No gracious weight of golden fruits to sell
Have I, nor any wise and wintry thing;
And I have loved you all too long and well
To carry still the high sweet breast of Spring.
Wherefore I say: O love, as summer goes,
I must be gone, steal forth with silent drums,
That you may hail anew the bird and rose
When I come back to you, as summer comes.
Else will you seek, at some not distant time,
Even your summer in another clime.

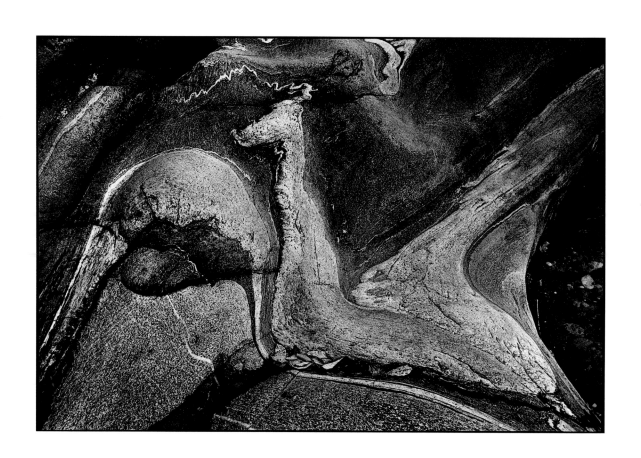

Ragged Island

There, there where those black spruces crowd
To the edge of the precipitous cliff,
Above your boat, under the eastern wall of the island;
And no wave breaks; as if
All had been done, and long ago, that needed
Doing; and the cold tide, unimpeded
By shoal or shelving ledge, moves up and down,
Instead of in and out;
And there is no driftwood there, because there is no beach;
Clean cliff going down as deep as clear water can reach;

No driftwood, such as abounds on the roaring shingle,
To be hefted home, for fires in the kitchen stove;
Barrels, banged ashore about the boiling outer harbour;
Lobster-buoys, on the eel-grass of the sheltered cove:

There, thought unbraids itself, and the mind becomes single.
There you row with tranquil oars, and the ocean
Shows no scar from the cutting of your placid keel;
Care becomes senseless there; pride and promotion
Remote; you only look; you scarcely feel.

Even adventure, with its vital uses,
Is aimless ardour now; and thrift is waste.

Oh, to be there, under the silent spruces,
Where the wide, quiet evening darkens without haste
Over a sea with death acquainted, yet forever chaste.

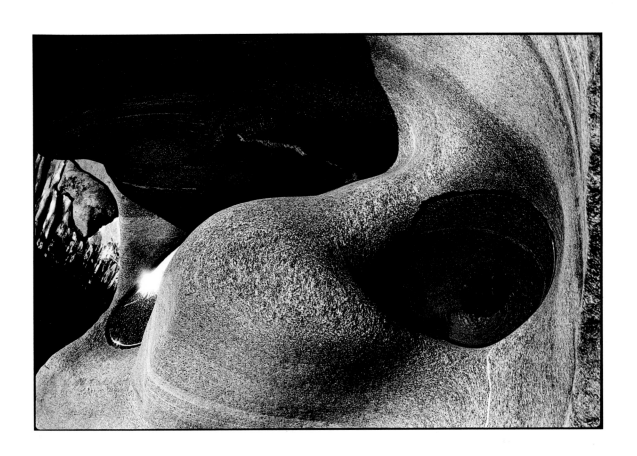

*   *   *

Into the golden vessel of great song
Let us pour all our passion; breast to breast
Let other lovers lie, in love and rest;
Not we,—articulate, so, but with the tongue
Of all the world: the churning blood, the long
Shuddering quiet, the desperate hot palms pressed
Sharply together upon the escaping guest,
The common soul, unguarded, and grown strong.
Longing alone is singer to the lute;
Let still on nettles in the open sigh
The minstrel, that in slumber is as mute
As any man, and love be far and high,
That else forsakes the topmost branch, a fruit
Found on the ground by every passer-by.

* * *

I, being born a woman and distressed
By all the needs and notions of my kind,
Am urged by your propinquity to find
Your person fair, and feel a certain zest
To bear your body's weight upon my breast:
So subtly is the fume of life designed,
To clarify the pulse and cloud the mind,
And leave me once again undone, possessed.
Think not for this, however, the poor treason
Of my stout blood against my staggering brain,
I shall remember you with love, or season
My scorn with pity, — let me make it plain:
I find this frenzy insufficient reason
For conversation when we meet again.

Travel

The railroad track is miles away,
    And the day is loud with voices speaking,
Yet there isn't a train goes by all day
    But I hear its whistle shrieking.

All night there isn't a train goes by,
    Though the night is still for sleep and dreaming,
But I see its cinders red on the sky,
    And hear its engine steaming.

My heart is warm with the friends I make,
    And better friends I'll not be knowing;
Yet there isn't a train I wouldn't take,
    No matter where it's going.

The Philosopher

And what are you that, wanting you,
   I should be kept awake
As many nights as there are days
   With weeping for your sake?

And what are you that, missing you,
   As many days as crawl
I should be listening to the wind
   And looking at the wall?

I know a man that's a braver man
   And twenty men as kind,
And what are you, that you should be
   The one man in my mind?

Yet women's ways are witless ways,
   As any sage will tell, —
And what am I, that I should love
   So wisely and so well?

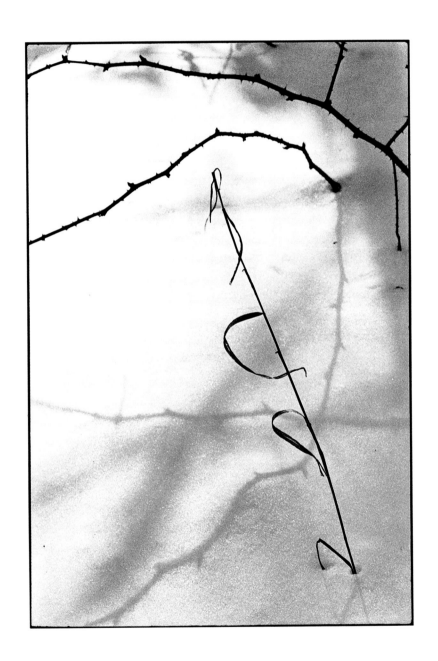

The True Encounter

"Wolf!" cried my cunning heart
   At every sheep it spied,
   And roused the countryside.

"Wolf! Wolf!"—and up would start
   Good neighbours, bringing spade
   And pitchfork to my aid.

At length my cry was known:
   Therein lay my release.
I met the wolf alone
   And was devoured in peace.

* * *

Not that it matters, not that my heart's cry
Is potent to deflect our common doom,
Or bind to truce in this ambiguous room
The planets of the atom as they ply;
But only to record that you and I,
Like thieves that scratch the jewels from a tomb,
Have gathered delicate love in hardy bloom
Close under Chaos, — I rise to testify.
This is my testament: that we are taken;
Our colours are as clouds before the wind;
Yet for a moment stood the foe forsaken,
Eyeing Love's favour to our helmet pinned;
Death is our master, — but his seat is shaken;
He rides victorious, — but his ranks are thinned.

Lines for a Grave-Stone

Man alive, that mournst thy lot,
Desiring what thou hast not got,
Money, beauty, love, what not;

Deeming it blesseder to be
A rotted man, than live to see
So rude a sky as covers thee;

Deeming thyself of all unblest
And wretched souls the wretchedest,
Longing to die and be at rest;

Know: that however grim the fate
Which sent thee forth to meditate
Upon my enviable state,

Here lieth one who would resign
Gladly his lot, to shoulder thine.
Give me thy coat; get into mine.

To the Not Impossible Him

How shall I know, unless I go
   To Cairo and Cathay,
Whether or not this blessed spot
   Is blest in every way?

Now it may be, the flower for me
   Is this beneath my nose;
How shall I tell, unless I smell
   The Carthaginian rose?

The fabric of my faithful love
   No power shall dim or ravel
Whilst I stay here,—but oh, my dear,
   If I should ever travel!

My Heart, Being Hungry

My heart, being hungry, feeds on food
   The fat of heart despise.
Beauty where beauty never stood,
   And sweet where no sweet lies
I gather to my querulous need,
Having a growing heart to feed.

It may be, when my heart is dull,
   Having attained its girth,
I shall not find so beautiful
   The meagre shapes of earth,
Nor linger in the rain to mark
The smell of tansy through the dark.

                    *   *   *

I pray you if you love me, bear my joy
A little while, or let me weep your tears;
I, too, have seen the quavering Fate destroy
Your destiny's bright spinning—the dull shears
Meeting not neatly, chewing at the thread,—
Nor can you well be less aware how fine,
How staunch as wire, and how unwarranted
Endures the golden fortune that is mine.
I pray you for this day at least, my dear,
Fare by my side, that journey in the sun;
Else must I turn me from the blossoming year
And walk in grief the way that you have gone.
Let us go forth together to the spring:
Love must be this, if it be anything.

Weeds

White with daisies and red with sorrel
   And empty, empty under the sky!—
Life is a quest and love a quarrel—
   Here is a place for me to lie.

Daisies spring from damned seeds,
   And this red fire that here I see
Is a worthless crop of crimson weeds,
   Cursed by farmers thriftily.

But here, unhated for an hour,
   The sorrel runs in ragged flame,
The daisy stands, a bastard flower,
   Like flowers that bear an honest name.

And here a while, where no wind brings
   The baying of a pack athirst,
May sleep the sleep of blessed things,
   The blood too bright, the brow accurst.

＊　　　＊　　　＊

I shall go back again to the bleak shore
And build a little shanty on the sand,
In such a way that the extremest band
Of brittle seaweed will escape my door
But by a yard or two; and nevermore
Shall I return to take you by the hand;
I shall be gone to what I understand,
And happier than I ever was before.
The love that stood a moment in your eyes,
The words that lay a moment on your tongue,
Are one with all that in a moment dies,
A little under-said and over-sung.
But I shall find the sullen rocks and skies
Unchanged from what they were when I was young.

Passer Mortuus Est

Death devours all lovely things:
　　Lesbia with her sparrow
Shares the darkness, — presently
　　Every bed is narrow.

Unremembered as old rain
　　Dries the sheer libation;
And the little petulant hand
　　Is an annotation.

After all, my erstwhile dear,
　　My no longer cherished,
Need we say it was not love,
　　Just because it perished?

Scrub

If I grow bitterly,
Like a gnarled and stunted tree,
Bearing harshly of my youth
Puckered fruit that sears the mouth;
If I make of my drawn boughs
An inhospitable house,
Out of which I never pry
Towards the water and the sky,
Under which I stand and hide
And hear the day go by outside;
It is that a wind too strong
Bent my back when I was young,
It is that I fear the rain
Lest it blister me again.

Truce for a Moment

Truce for a moment between Earth and Ether
Slackens the mind's allegiance to despair:
 Shyly confer earth, water, fire and air
With the fifth essence.

For the duration, if the mind require it,
Trigged is the wheel of Time against the slope;
Infinite Space lies curved within the scope
Of the hand's cradle.

Thus between day and evening in the autumn,
High in the west alone and burning bright,
Venus has hung, the earliest riding-light
In the calm harbour.

Epitaph for the Race of Man

IV

O Earth, unhappy planet born to die,
Might I your scribe and your confessor be,
What wonders must you not relate to me
Of Man, who when his destiny was high
Strode like the sun into the middle sky
And shone an hour, and who so bright as he,
And like the sun went down into the sea,
Leaving no spark to be remembered by.
But no; you have not learned in all these years
To tell the leopard and the newt apart;
Man, with his singular laughter, his droll tears,
His engines and his conscience and his art,
Made but a simple sound upon your ears:
The patient beating of the animal heart.

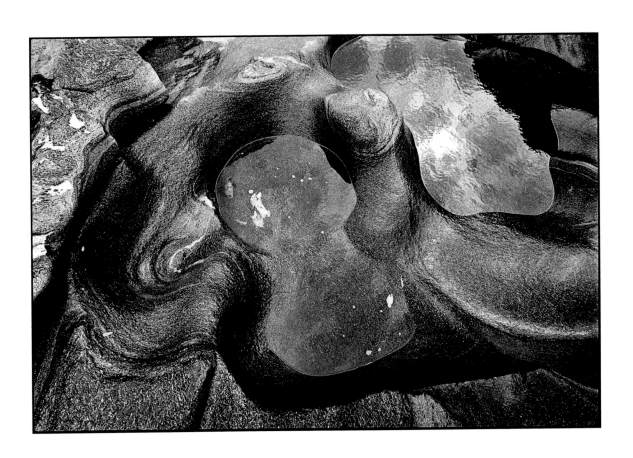

Epitaph for the Race of Man

V

When Man is gone and only gods remain
To stride the world, their mighty bodies hung
With golden shields, and golden curls outflung
Above their childish foreheads; when the plain
Round skull of Man is lifted and again
Abandoned by the ebbing wave, among
The sand and pebbles of the beach, — what tongue
Will tell the marvel of the human brain?
Heavy with music once this windy shell,
Heavy with knowledge of the clustered stars;
The one-time tenant of this draughty hall
Himself, in learned pamphlet, did foretell,
After some aeons of study jarred by wars,
This toothy gourd, this head emptied of all.

Mortal Flesh, Is Not Your Place in the Ground?

Mortal flesh, is not your place in the ground? — Why do you stare so
At the bright planet serene in the clear green evening sky above
    the many-coloured streaked clouds? —
Your brows drawn together as if to chide, your mouth set as if in anger.

Learn to love blackness while there is yet time, blackness
Unpatterned, blackness without horizons.

Beautiful are the trees in autumn, the emerald pines
Dark among the light-red leaves of the maple and the dark-red
Leaves of the white oak and the indigo long
Leaves of the white ash.
But why do you stand so, staring with stern face of ecstasy
    at the autumn leaves,
At the boughs hung with banners along the road as if a procession
    were about to pass?

Learn to love roots instead, that soon above your head
    shall be as branches.

Counting-out Rhyme

Silver bark of beech, and sallow
Bark of yellow birch and yellow
   Twig of willow.

Stripe of green in moosewood maple,
Colour seen in leaf of apple,
   Bark of popple.

Wood of popple pale as moonbeam,
Wood of oak for yoke and barn-beam,
   Wood of hornbeam.

Silver bark of beech, and hollow
Stem of elder, tall and yellow
   Twig of willow.

Pastoral

If it were only still! —
With far away the shrill
Crying of a cock;
Or the shaken bell
From a cow's throat
Moving through the bushes;
Or the soft shock
Of wizened apples falling
From an old tree
In a forgotten orchard
Upon the hilly rock!

Oh, grey hill,
Where the grazing herd
Licks the purple blossom,
Crops the spiky weed!
Oh, stony pasture,
Where the tall mullein
Stands up so sturdy
On its little seed!

City Trees

The trees along this city street,
   Save for the traffic and the trains,
Would make a sound as thin and sweet
   As trees in country lanes.

And people standing in their shade
   Out of a shower, undoubtedly
Would hear such music as is made
   Upon a country tree.

Oh, little leaves that are so dumb
   Against the shrieking city air,
I watch you when the wind has come, —
   I know what sound is there.

First Fig

My candle burns at both ends;
   It will not last the night;
But ah, my foes, and oh, my friends—
   It gives a lovely light!

Second Fig

Safe upon the solid rock the ugly houses stand:
Come and see my shining palace built upon the sand!

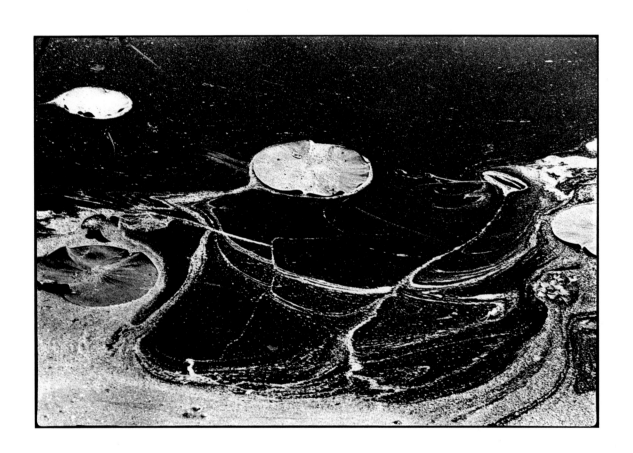

Tranquility at length, when autumn comes,
Will lie upon the spirit like that haze
Touching far islands on fine autumn days
With tenderest blue, like bloom on purple plums;
Harvest will ring, but not as summer hums,
With noisy enterprise—to broaden, raise,
Proceed, proclaim, establish: autumn stays
The marching year one moment; stills the drums.
Then sits the insistent cricket in the grass;
But on the gravel crawls the chilly bee;
And all is over that could come to pass
Last year; excepting this: the mind is free
One moment, to compute, refute, amass,
Catalogue, question, contemplate, and see.

Mariposa

Butterflies are white and blue
In this field we wander through.
Suffer me to take your hand.
Death comes in a day or two.

All the things we ever knew
Will be ashes in that hour:
Mark the transient butterfly,
How he hangs upon the flower.

Suffer me to take your hand.
Suffer me to cherish you
Till the dawn is in the sky.
Whether I be false or true,
Death comes in a day or two.

Sonnet

Time, that renews the tissues of this frame,
That built the child and hardened the soft bone,
Taught him to wail, to blink, to walk alone,
Stare, question, wonder, give the world a name,
Forget the watery darkness whence he came,
Attends no less the boy to manhood grown,
Brings him new raiment, strips him of his own:
All skins are shed at length, remorse, even shame.
Such hope is mine, if this indeed be true,
I dread no more the first white in my hair,
Or even age itself, the easy shoe,
The cane, the wrinkled hands, the special chair:
Time, doing this to me, may alter too
My anguish, into something I can bear.

To Inez Milholland

*Read in Washington, November eighteenth, 1923, at the unveiling
of a statue of three leaders in the cause of Equal Rights for Women*

Upon this marble bust that is not I

Lay the round, formal wreath that is not fame;

But in the forum of my silenced cry

Root ye the living tree whose sap is flame.

I, that was proud and valiant, am no more;—

Save as a dream that wanders wide and late,

Save as a wind that rattles the stout door,

Troubling the ashes in the sheltered grate.

The stone will perish; I shall be twice dust.

Only my standard on a taken hill

Can cheat the mildew and the red-brown rust

And make immortal my adventurous will.

Even now the silk is tugging at the staff:

Take up the song; forget the epitaph.